Mysteries
OF THE
PYRAMIDS

© Aladdin Books Ltd 1995

Designed and produced by
Aladdin Books Ltd
28 Percy Street
London W1P 0LD

ISBN 0 7496 1950 3

First published in Britain in 1995 by
Aladdin Books/Watts Books
96 Leonard Street
London EC2A 4RH

The author, Dr Anne Millard, has a PhD in Egyptology from University College, London. She is the author of numerous books on ancient Egypt and other aspects of the ancient world.

The consultant, George Hart, is an Egyptologist working at the Education Section of the British Museum, London. He has written extensively on ancient Egyptian books and pyramids.

Editor: Katie Roden

Design: **David West** • CHILDREN'S BOOK DESIGN

Designer: Flick Killerby

Picture Research: Brooks Krikler Research

Illustrators: Francis Phillipps,
Stephen Sweet: Simon Girling and Associates, Rob Shone

Printed in Belgium

Mysteries
OF THE
PYRAMIDS

Anne Millard

ALADDIN/WATTS
LONDON · SYDNEY

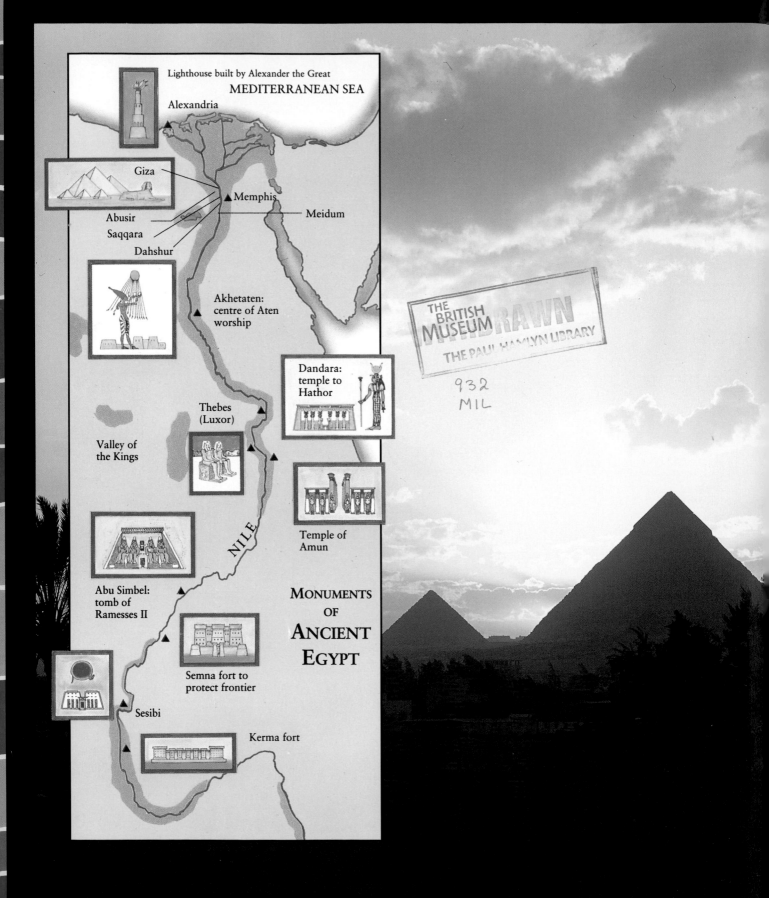

Lighthouse built by Alexander the Great

MEDITERRANEAN SEA

Alexandria

Giza

Memphis

Abusir

Saqqara

Meidum

Dahshur

Akhetaten:
centre of Aten
worship

Dandara:
temple to
Hathor

Thebes
(Luxor)

Valley of
the Kings

Temple of
Amun

NILE

Abu Simbel:
tomb of
Ramesses II

Monuments
of
Ancient
Egypt

Semna fort to
protect frontier

Sesibi

Kerma fort

CONTENTS

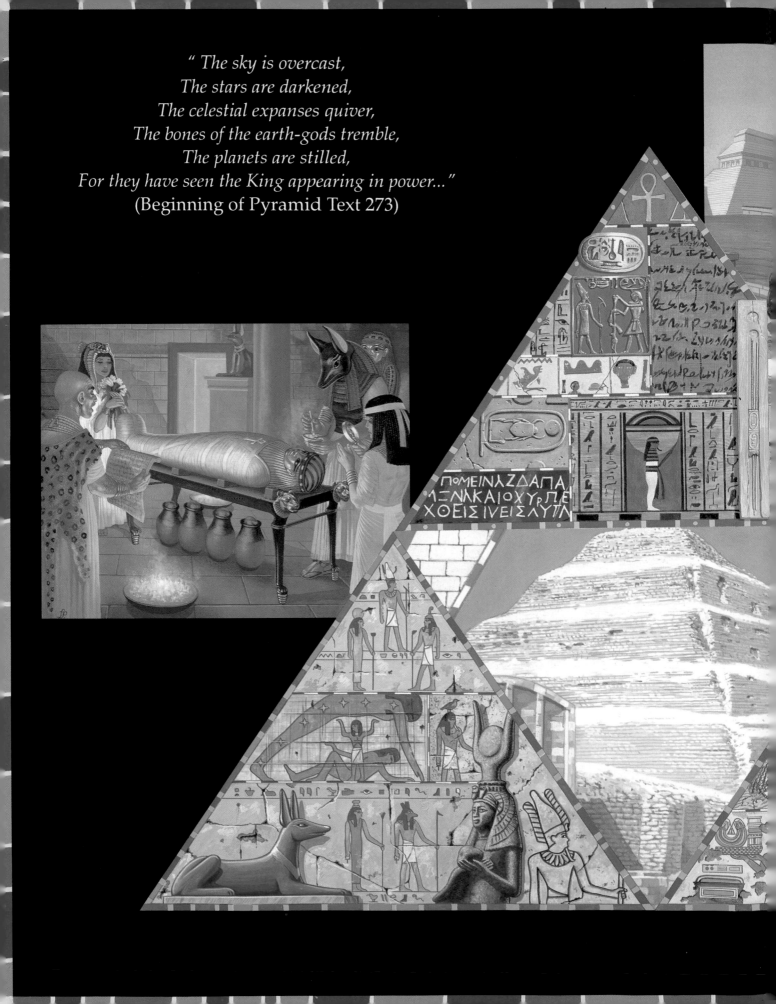

" *The sky is overcast,*
The stars are darkened,
The celestial expanses quiver,
The bones of the earth-gods tremble,
The planets are stilled,
For they have seen the King appearing in power..."
(Beginning of Pyramid Text 273)

Introduction to THE MYSTERIES

They stand silent and mysterious on the Giza Plateau in Egypt – three mighty pyramids and six smaller ones. Meanwhile, across the world, vast pyramid-like structures tower above the rainforests of Central and South America – monuments of great empires which have now disappeared for ever.

There are over three dozen Kings' pyramids in Egypt, but as the centuries passed, all knowledge of their royal history was lost. People came up with some weird and wonderful ideas, believing that the pyramids were anything from ancient observatories to the work of visitors from outer space! It was not until the nineteenth century AD that the pyramids were examined in great detail. Since the age of the first explorers, lots of puzzles have been solved, but modern science still cannot explain many mysteries. In the last few years a French team and a Japanese team have both claimed to have evidence that there are other chambers in the Great Pyramid at Giza, unopened since the days of Khufu over 4,000 years ago. What secrets might these chambers reveal? Will they help us to understand the great civilisation of ancient Egypt?

"To take a better footing we put off our shoes and most of our apparel, foretold of the heat within, not inferior to a stove. Our guide went foremost, everyone with our lights in our hands. A most dreadful passage...not above a yard in breadth and four foot in height...so always stooping and sometimes creeping." (early explorer)

The First
EXPLORERS

If you visit a pyramid today, you will find electric lights, steps to climb and rails to help you find your way. When early explorers entered, 300 years ago, they had only flickering candlelight and the strong hands of their guides to lead them into the intense heat and fearsome darkness of the pyramids. There was a terrible stench and the air was thick with dust. But these intrepid explorers braved the heat and the possible danger, and had many adventures.

The first tourists to visit the Giza pyramids were the ancient Egyptians themselves, then the Greeks and Romans. After the Arab invasion of Egypt in AD 639, the outer stones from the pyramids were used to build the city of Cairo. For centuries, very few people could visit Egypt, so scholars had little information about the pyramids. Were these wonderful monuments just tombs? Surely they had other uses?

Early Explorers
AND DISCOVERERS

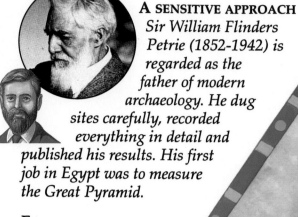

Throughout history, people have tried to understand the pyramids. Early Christians thought they were places where priests watched the stars. In the nineteenth century, some people believed that the measurements of the Great Pyramid were inspired by God, and that from them they could predict the future! But by then, scholars could read ancient Egyptian writing and they had started to dig up historic sites. The pyramids were now known to be the last resting places of Egypt's early Kings.

A SENSITIVE APPROACH
Sir William Flinders Petrie (1852-1942) is regarded as the father of modern archaeology. He dug sites carefully, recorded everything in detail and published his results. His first job in Egypt was to measure the Great Pyramid.

EARLY ADVENTURER
Jean de Thevenot (1633-67, below) was one of the first explorers of ancient Egyptian sites.

THE BURIED SPHINX
In Egyptian legend, the Sphinx (the statue which guards the pyramids) appeared to a prince in a dream. It promised to make him King if he would clear the sand from its body. He did so, and became Tuthmosis IV.

NAPOLEON'S NIGHTMARE
Napoleon Bonaparte, the Emperor of France, led an invasion of Egypt in 1798. Legend has it that he ventured into the Great Pyramid alone, only to emerge pale, shaken and gasping for air. What secrets did he encounter in the darkness? We will never know...

TREASURE HUNTERS

In the early nineteenth century, great damage was done by collectors and their agents. They entered the tombs in all sorts of ways, including blasting their way in. Giovanni Belzoni was a former circus strong-man, who was hired by a collector to gather ancient Egyptian artefacts. He had no idea of preservation – one of his writings describes how he clumsily crushed Late Period mummies as he forced his way into a tomb.

Preserving the treasures

Many museums and universities have excavated sites in Egypt. The objects found are treated by experts, then stored for future research. X-rays, medical scanners (below), robot photography and other modern techniques are used to help scientists understand the secrets of the tombs.

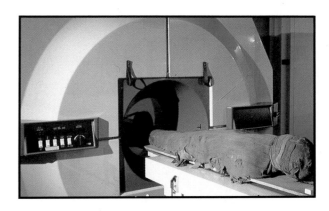

PYRAMID GRAFFITI

Belzoni even carved his name on the stones of the pyramids!

When did tourists start to arrive?
In 1869, Thomas Cook, a British travel agent, bought a paddle-steamer in Egypt and offered a new service – a package holiday. He charged one amount to cover everything – travel to Egypt, a Nile cruise and a guide. Until then, visitors to Egypt had to arrange all these details for themselves, which could often be very difficult and extremely expensive.

UNCHARTED TERRITORY

After the Arab invasion of Egypt, few people were able to visit the country. Little was known about the pyramids, the Nile Valley and its surroundings, or the culture and history of ancient Egypt.

Reading the
HIEROGLYPHS

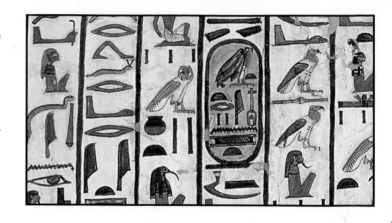

The Egyptians had invented a picture writing that we call hieroglyphs by about 3000 BC. Some of their signs were single letters. Others had the value of two, three or more letters. The signs were combined to form words. Hieroglyphs take a long time to write, so the Egyptians invented a 'short-hand' script which we call hieratic, and another, demotic, about 2,500 years later. These were used in daily life, and hieroglyphs were kept for religious texts only. For centuries, no one could read the hieroglyphs, but in 1822 a great breakthrough was made...

THE ROYAL CARTOUCHE
To emphasise and protect royal or holy names, the Egyptians wrote them in a frame called a cartouche (above). Champollion (see below) used cartouches on the Rosetta Stone to help him translate the hieroglyphs. He read the one below in its Greek version. It was Ptolemy, a ruler of Egypt. He then worked out which hieroglyphs spelt the name.

| P | | O | L | | Y | S |
| T | | | M | | | |

* no translation

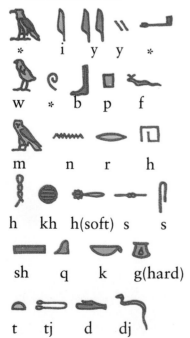

	i	y	y	
*	i	y	y	*
w	*	b	p	f
m	n	r	h	
h	kh	h(soft)	s	s
sh	q	k	g(hard)	
t	tj	d	dj	

FINDING THE KEY
The Rosetta Stone is carved in hieroglyphs, demotic and Greek. It was discovered in Egypt in 1799.

CRACKING THE CODE
In 1822, a brilliant young French scholar, called Jean François Champollion, used his knowledge of ancient Greek to read the Rosetta Stone. He had translated the mysterious hieroglyphs at last.

NEW TEXTS

The last hieroglyphic inscription was carved in Philae temple in AD 394. Old Egyptian writing then died out. Instead, people used an alphabet called Coptic. The name comes from an Arabic word, gubti, based on the ancient Greek name for Egypt.

Demotic text

Scribe's palette

Ancient maths

The Egyptians also used symbols for their numbers. Can you write 2,375 in Egyptian numerals?

1	10	100	1,000
10,000	100,000	1,000,000	

ANSWER:

WRITING PAPER

As well as carving and painting hieroglyphs on walls and stone tablets, the Egyptians also used paper made from papyrus, a type of reed (below). The inside part of the papyrus stem was cut into strips and was made into long sheets of paper by soaking and pressing. Many papyri have survived to this day, preserved by the hot sun and sand of Egypt.

HEAVENLY GUIDE BOOKS

In the pyramid of the last King of Dynasty V and in all Dynasty VI pyramids, we find writings called the Pyramid Texts. These were believed to help the King move easily into the Next World (heaven).

They contained prayers, pleas and ritual pronouncements to the gods. It was hoped that the gods, such as Anubis (left), would welcome the King and allow him to pass into the Next World to live a new, happy and everlasting life.

> "The fashioner of costly stones seeks for skill in every kind of hard stone. When he has fully completed things, his arms are destroyed and he is weary. When he sits down at the going in of Re [sunset], his thighs and his back are cramped."
> (from *The Satire of Trades*)

Building the PYRAMIDS

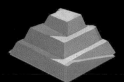

Why were the pyramids built? Who built them? How was it done? These questions puzzled the world for centuries, even after Champollion translated the hieroglyphs. It then became clear that the pyramids were tombs. The names of the Kings who had them built are inscribed or painted in the tombs, mixed with the names of the gangs of workers who built them, scrawled on the rocks.

Most Egyptian people were farmers. Egypt has very little rain, but water is supplied by the Nile. Every year the river flooded, covering the land for four months. During this time, the Inundation, the farmers could not tend their fields, so the King summoned them to work on his pyramid instead. This labour was a form of tax to the King. People usually went willingly, although the work was hard. They believed that the King was a god and would look after them in the Next World in return for their labour.

Construction AND LABOUR

When a suitably firm site had been chosen, the ground was flattened and the base of the pyramid was marked out. Building could then begin. The great stones were tied to wooden sledges and dragged into place, one at a time, by teams of workers. Finally, a white limestone casing was put on the pyramid.

BUILDING BLOCKS

Most of the stone for the pyramids came from local quarries, but the fine white limestone for the casing (right) came from Tura on the east bank of the Nile, and had to be floated across the river. Each block was then put on a wooden sledge and dragged into place by a gang of workers. To help the sledge run smoothly, the workers put wooden rollers on the ground in front of it. Water was poured continuously on to the rollers, so that the heat and friction caused by the movement of the enormous stone would not start a fire.

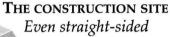

THE CONSTRUCTION SITE

Even straight-sided pyramids were built with a step pyramid inside them (top). To build the central structure, the stone blocks were probably dragged into place up ramps made of bricks and rubble (centre). One wide ramp (bottom) was used to add the outer casing. It was made longer and higher as the pyramid grew taller, and was taken apart when building ended.

How many blocks made a pyramid?
This depended on its size. The Great Pyramid contains about 2,300,000.
How much did each block weigh?
This also depended on size. Most Great Pyramid blocks were about 2.5 tonnes.

THE HOLY ARCHITECT

The designer of the first-ever pyramid was named Imhotep. In about 2700 BC he built a step pyramid for King Zoser. He was believed to be so wise, and his pyramid was so impressive, that he was later worshipped as a god!

The pyramid complex

On the edge of a complex was the Valley Temple, which was probably where the King's body was prepared for burial. A causeway (path) led to a Mortuary Temple, where offerings were made to the King's spirit. There was also a small pyramid for the Queen and rectangular tombs, or mastabas, for the royal family and the courtiers.

Mortuary Temple

GLEAMING WHITE
Originally, the pyramids were covered with fine white limestone (above). However, this was stolen over the centuries.

Causeway

Valley Temple

A HUGE WORKFORCE
Skilled stone masons, labourers and other craftspeople worked all year round on a pyramid, but most of the work was done during the four months of the Inundation, when the farmers arrived to do their labour tax. They were fed, housed and clothed by the King. It was an enormous feat to look after so many people – as many as 80,000 at one time – and to organise their work efficiently. The workers were paid in linen, beer and oil. They also received food including meat, fish, vegetables, fruit, cheese and a type of wholemeal bread.

TOOLS OF THE TRADE
The Old Kingdom pyramid builders had copper chisels and saws, and wooden sledges to pull the blocks. To carve the blocks from the quarries, wooden wedges were driven into the rock and soaked with water. The wood swelled, splitting the stone. Another method was to heat the rock then throw cold water over it, to make it crack.

Pyramids AND KINGS

Egypt's Kings were believed to be related to the gods and were treated with great respect. At first they were buried in rectangular, mud-brick tombs. But the great Imhotep decided that mud did not last long enough for royal burials, and built a stone mastaba for his ruler, Zoser. He made it bigger by putting another mastaba on top, then another and another...and the world's first step pyramid was born. King Huni built another step pyramid, but his son Sneferu made its sides straight. After that, all pyramids were built with straight sides.

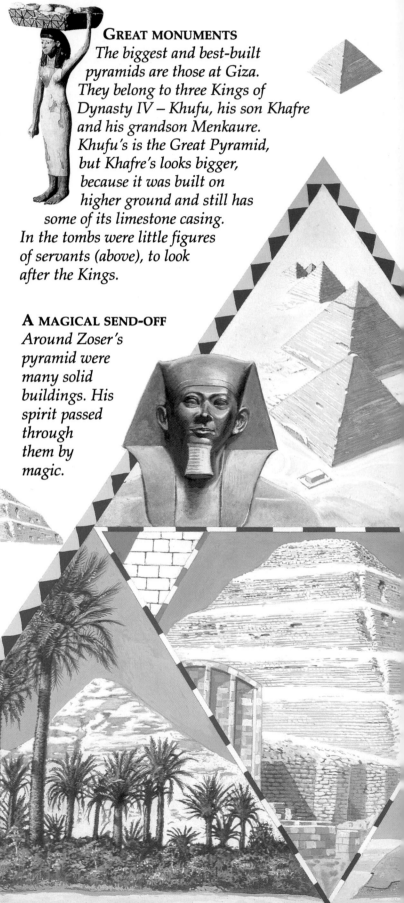

GREAT MONUMENTS
The biggest and best-built pyramids are those at Giza. They belong to three Kings of Dynasty IV – Khufu, his son Khafre and his grandson Menkaure. Khufu's is the Great Pyramid, but Khafre's looks bigger, because it was built on higher ground and still has some of its limestone casing. In the tombs were little figures of servants (above), to look after the Kings.

A MAGICAL SEND-OFF
Around Zoser's pyramid were many solid buildings. His spirit passed through them by magic.

THE ROYAL GRAVEYARD
The smaller, less well-built pyramids at Abusir and Saqqara belong to the Kings of Dynasties V and VI. These sites are packed full of tombs, dating from throughout the Egyptian period. The tombs include the pyramid of King Userkaf (right), with a colossal head of the ruler.

Did the pyramids ever go wrong?
The pyramid builders were usually very accurate. But everyone makes mistakes! King Sneferu built two pyramids at Dahshur, one of which is known as the Bent Pyramid. It was meant to be straight-sided, but when it had been partially built, the architects decided that its sides were too steep and it might collapse. It was finished with the sides sloping more gently at the bottom, so it looks bent.

A COMPLETE DISASTER
The Meidum Pyramid was the engineers' biggest blunder. At some point, all the outer casing fell off, dragging most of the insides down with it. The engineers had built the new, straight-sided casing on a foundation of soft sand rather than hard rock.

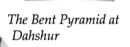

The Bent Pyramid at Dahshur

Zoser (right), a god-King of Egypt

A class of its own

The Great Pyramid is unlike any other pyramid, with three main chambers rather than one. Were these changes designed to trick grave robbers? The highest chamber is the only burial chamber, where the King lay.

The Great Pyramid at Giza

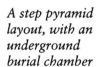

A step pyramid layout, with an underground burial chamber

The lower one is called the 'Queen's chamber', but the Queen was buried in her own small pyramid. There are four tiny shafts in the King's and Queen's chambers. Many people think they were built to let the royal spirits reach the stars. Most other pyramids are simpler, with one central burial chamber and two or three antechambers.

"Oh King, you have not departed dead, you have departed alive!...Raise yourself up, oh King! Receive your head, collect your bones, gather your limbs together..."
(Pyramid Text)

A Life after DEATH

The Egyptians believed that the only way they could properly enjoy life in the Next World was if their bodies survived. Even the King's body had to last, in case he needed it, although his soul travelled to the Next World to live with his godly relatives.

In early Egypt, people were buried in shallow graves in the desert sand. This dried and preserved their bodies in a natural way. However, once the Egyptians put their Kings and nobles in splendid tombs, the bodies decayed easily, and artificial ways of preserving them were invented. The most successful method – called mummification – was at its peak in the New Kingdom. The internal organs (lungs, brain, liver etc) were taken out and the body was covered with a salt called natron, which dried it out. It was then stuffed with linen and resin and wrapped in hundreds of metres of linen. Many bodies have been almost perfectly preserved.

Preparing for THE AFTERLIFE

It sometimes seems that the ancient Egyptians spent most of their time thinking about death, but this isn't true. They loved their life on earth so much that they believed the Next World would be like Egypt, but without sadness, worries or suffering. They therefore went to great trouble to prepare for their eternal life and to make sure they would have a good time. This meant building a comfortable tomb, full of all the furniture and belongings they might need. Above all, they made sure they would have regular supplies of food, drink and entertainment.

SOULS AND SPIRITS
The Egyptians believed they had three spirits – the ka, ba and akh. The ka was the life force of a person. After death it lived in the tomb, and was kept comfortable with offerings and model servants (right). The ba represented the personality. It was shown as a human-headed bird, but it could change shape and leave the tomb. The akh (written as a crested ibis) went to join the stars or Osiris.

MEMORY AIDS
Mummies were decorated with an image of the dead, so the ba recognised the body. Mirrors and combs enabled the dead to look their best.

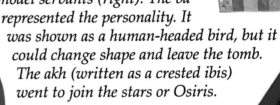

HEAVENLY PLEASURES
Paintings of food and entertainers (below) were often placed in tombs, to keep the souls happy.

Why are mummies called mummies?
The Arabs thought bitumen was used in embalming, so called mummies after their word for bitumen, mummiya.

WEALTH AND RICHES
Jewellery and treasures were usually put in the tombs of both men and women. Even the poorest people were buried with some jewellery, to make sure they looked impressive in their new life with the gods and goddesses.

HEAVENLY SERVANTS
Little servant figures, or shabtis (right), were placed in the tomb, to help the dead person in the Next World.

Grave robbers

Everyone knew that great riches were placed in royal tombs. While guards watched over the burial places, these treasures were safe. But over the centuries the tombs were no longer guarded, and thieves broke in – even though they knew it insulted the gods. If they were caught they would be executed, but this did not put them off!

LONG LIFE
The organs were preserved and put in containers called canopic jars.

SAILING IN THE SKY
In some dynasties, model boats were placed in the tombs. They represented the boat that carried dead people over the Nile to the Next World.

Full-sized boats have been found in several tombs at Giza. They were probably used by the King in life, and to carry his dead body over the Nile to his final resting place.

Joining the GODS

In the Old Kingdom, the chief god was the sun-god Re, who sailed across the sky every day in a boat. His children were Tefnut (Moisture) and Shu (Air). They were the parents of Geb (Earth) and Nut (Sky), whose children were Osiris, his wife Isis, Set, the lord of desert and storms, Nephthys his wife, and the stars. Set murdered his brother Osiris, cut up his body and threw the pieces into the Nile. Isis and Nephthys gathered up the pieces and brought Osiris back to life, helped by Anubis. When a King died, he went to the heavens to join the gods.

WEIGHING YOUR CHANCES
Anubis (below) was the guardian of the dead. He held the scales of justice. People had to prove that they were worthy of joining Osiris (right) by having their heart weighed against the Feather of Truth (above). If the scales balanced, a person had led a good life. A bad heart would tip the scales and he or she would be thrown to a terrible monster, the Devourer.

IMAGES OF THE GODS
Gods like Geb (bottom centre) and Shu (above right) were believed to have beards. Kings (and Queens who ruled as Kings) wore false beards to show their closeness to the gods.

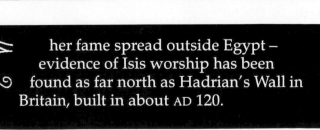

Which deity had the most power? Isis, the loving mother of all, had more magic power than any other god or goddess. In ancient Roman times, her fame spread outside Egypt – evidence of Isis worship has been found as far north as Hadrian's Wall in Britain, built in about AD 120.

Sacred pets

The Egyptians wanted to be close to their gods and goddesses, but no living person was allowed to look on them. Therefore a special animal or bird was chosen to represent each deity. The spirit of the god or goddess would enter the creature's body, and so could be near his or her worshippers and bring them comfort. Cats were especially popular, and many animals were mummified like their owners.

HORUS

Horus, the son of the deities Isis (right) and Osiris, fought his evil uncle Set (below) then went on to become the King of Egypt. In the desperate fight against Set, the left eye of Horus was plucked out. The eye of Horus came to symbolise sacrifice and offerings to the dead. The moon was also believed to be Horus' left eye. Horus was usually portrayed as a falcon (left) in traditional ancient Egyptian mythology and art.

TEMPLE WORSHIP

Huge temples were built as homes for the gods and goddesses on earth. Only priests, priestesses and royalty could enter the temples.

Ordinary people worshipped at home. The deity's statue was kept in a shrine, and was brought out daily to be cleaned, dressed and worshipped with prayers.

> "A stairway to the sky is set up for me that I may ascend to the sky..."
>
> "May the sky make the sunlight strong for you, may you rise up to the sky..."
>
> (Pyramid Texts 284, 523)

New Ideas and INVESTIGATIONS

The pyramid was the place where the King's body and possessions were buried, and where offerings were supposed to be made to him for ever. But it was also the place where the god-King's spirit was launched to the heavens to join his relatives, the gods and goddesses.

Most experts agree that the souls of the early Kings were believed to be heading for the stars. Step pyramids were stairways to the stars, and straight-sided pyramids were like sunbeams made of stone, which the King could climb to reach Re.

But the pyramids may have had many more uses. Does the pyramid also represent a mound, which in Egyptian creation stories was the first land to appear from the original watery nothingness? Does the layout of the Giza pyramids imitate the position of the main stars in the groups we call Orion and Sirius? How can we explain several missing mummies and empty tombs?

Secrets of
THE STARS

The movements of the sun, moon and stars were important in Egyptian religion, and the Egyptian calendar was based on these movements. Each week was marked by a new group of stars rising in the sky at dawn. The Egyptians divided the stars into constellations (groups), but their groupings were different to ours. Maps of the heavens show the sun-god and stars crossing the sky in boats. This shows the importance of the Nile to the Egyptians.

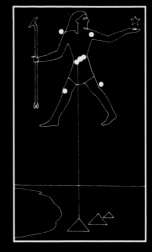

MAPPING THE STARS
The group of stars we call Orion (left) was called Sahu by the Egyptians. They believed that the soul of Osiris went there after he was murdered by his brother Set. Near Sahu/Osiris is the star we call Sirius, known to the Egyptians as Sopdet. They saw Sopdet as Isis, the wife of Osiris. Sopdet spends 70 days a year below the horizon, invisible from Egypt. Its return to view marked the Egyptian New Year. The Nile flood came at that time, and was thought to be Isis weeping for Osiris.

STARRY GODS
Many temples were decorated with constellation gods (right) and star deities.

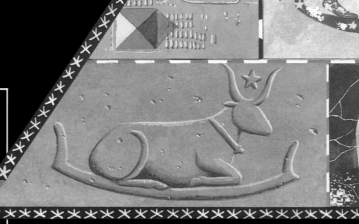

HEAVENLY BIRDS

In the Old Kingdom, swallows (left) were identified with the stars. They heralded the dawn, and were often shown on the front of Re's sun-boat. In later images, the head of a falcon was often shown descending from the sky. It represented the sun's rays and the eye of Horus.

HOLY COW
The cow (right) was the sacred animal of the goddess Hathor, the Queen of Heaven.

How did the Egyptian calendar work? The Egyptian week had 10 days. 3 weeks made a month and 12 months a year. There were 5 holy days at the end of the year, making 365 days.

THE SACRED SKY
The sky hieroglyph (above) shows the heavens as a solid ceiling, and was often used above doorways.

A VIEW OF THE WORLD
The sun was believed to be the right eye of the god Horus.

THE LOVE OF THE GODS
The Egyptians believed that the sky was the goddess Nut (below), stretching her body over the earth. In Egyptian mythology, Nut married Geb, the earth-god, but Re was opposed to their marriage and ordered their father, Shu, to push them apart for eternity. However, by this time Geb and Nut had already become the parents of the stars and of the four great deities.

THE DIVINE STARS
The northern stars were always visible, so were called 'The Imperishable Ones'.

Mysteries of the heavens

What are the four narrow shafts that lead out of the burial chambers in Khufu's pyramid? Recently it was discovered that one of the two shafts in the King's chamber points to the northern stars, which never sink below the horizon. The other points to Orion. Was this a passage for the dead King's soul to reach Osiris quickly? It is also suggested that the Queen's chamber shafts point to the stars. One faces Sirius – could this be another passageway to the heavens?

Orion/
Sahu/
Osiris

Sirius/
Sopdet/
Isis

The Giza pyramids are not quite in a straight line. The Egyptologist Robert Bauval claims they are laid out like the three main stars of Orion/Sahu/ Osiris and that they were built for astronomical as well as religious reasons.

Puzzles and MYSTERIES

In the Middle Ages (5th-15th centuries AD), the pyramids were said to have been grain stores, then were believed to have been early observatories. In the nineteenth century, one theory said that the Great Pyramid's measurements were inspired by God and contained a code that could predict all the main events of world history! Even today, crazy ideas about the the pyramids are still popular, but new evidence and theories are constantly improving our understanding of these huge, mysterious monuments.

A SECRET CHAMBER?

In 1994, a team of scientists sent a tiny robot, called UPUAUT II, up the narrow southern shaft of the Queen's chamber of Khufu's pyramid. They wanted to see if they could ventilate the pyramid better, because of the number of tourists visiting it every year. The robot travelled about 60 metres...then its TV camera showed a slab of stone with copper handles blocking its way. What lies behind this tiny door? Could there be a hidden chamber? What might it contain – a statue, hidden writings, wonderful treasures...or nothing at all? Scientists are hoping to look through a crack at the base of the stone with a tiny camera, the type that is used by doctors to see inside patients. What will it reveal?

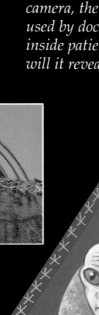

AN ANCIENT PUZZLE

Archaeologists believe that the Sphinx was carved from stone left in a quarry when the pyramids were completed. Yet one man has a theory that it is thousands of years older than the pyramids. He says that the wind and rain have worn away its face much more than the surface of the pyramids, so he claims it was the work of an earlier civilisation. This is pretty unlikely, because no other traces of such a civilisation have been found.

EXTRA-TERRESTRIAL EGYPTIANS

There are even people who suggest that the pyramids were built by aliens!

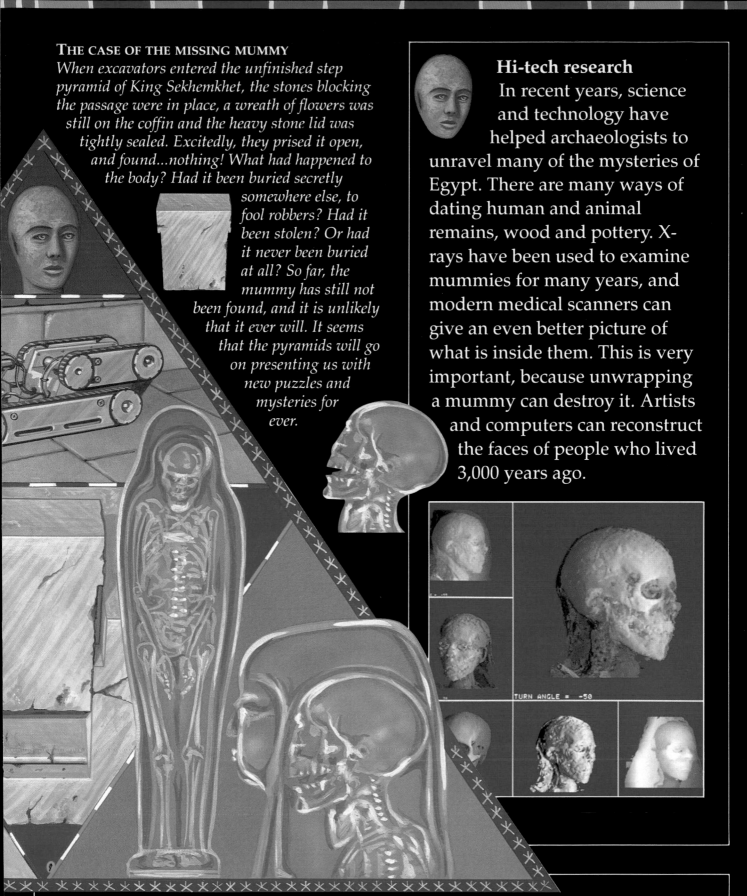

THE CASE OF THE MISSING MUMMY

When excavators entered the unfinished step pyramid of King Sekhemkhet, the stones blocking the passage were in place, a wreath of flowers was still on the coffin and the heavy stone lid was tightly sealed. Excitedly, they prised it open, and found...nothing! What had happened to the body? Had it been buried secretly somewhere else, to fool robbers? Had it been stolen? Or had it never been buried at all? So far, the mummy has still not been found, and it is unlikely that it ever will. It seems that the pyramids will go on presenting us with new puzzles and mysteries for ever.

Hi-tech research

In recent years, science and technology have helped archaeologists to unravel many of the mysteries of Egypt. There are many ways of dating human and animal remains, wood and pottery. X-rays have been used to examine mummies for many years, and modern medical scanners can give an even better picture of what is inside them. This is very important, because unwrapping a mummy can destroy it. Artists and computers can reconstruct the faces of people who lived 3,000 years ago.

TURN ANGLE = -50

What did the Egyptians look like? Archaeologists use police techniques to recreate faces from ancient skulls, using computer graphics or clay.

"The usual method of sacrifice was to open the victim's chest, pull out his heart while he was still half alive, and then knock down the man, rolling him down the temple steps which were awash with blood."
(José de Acosta, *Natural and Moral History of the Indies*, 1590)

Pyramids around THE WORLD

The Egyptians were not the only civilisation to build great pyramid-shaped structures. The ancient peoples of Mesopotamia (now eastern Syria, southeastern Turkey and most of Iraq) built pyramid shapes to bring themselves closer to their gods and goddesses. They constructed mud-brick platforms, with temples to house the gods on the flat tops. There the priests sent offerings and prayers to the gods. We call these temple platforms ziggurats.

In North, Central and South America, peoples such as the Aztecs and Incas also built flat-topped pyramids (left). People were sometimes buried under them, but they were not meant to be tombs. Temples were built on top of these pyramids, where sacrifices of food, animals and sometimes human beings were offered. Early Native American peoples built large, pyramid-shaped mounds in which to bury their dead, and to use as shrines.

Popular PYRAMIDS

Central and South America saw the rise and fall of many civilisations, such as the Olmecs, Toltecs, Maya, Incas and Aztecs, before the arrival of European settlers in the sixteenth century. These peoples first built great mounds of earth, then developed flat-topped pyramids by casing the mounds in stone with steep steps. These were places where gods and people could meet. The pyramids had temples on top, but some had burials underneath. The Europeans destroyed hundreds of ancient cities, and many treasures and artefacts were lost.

SACRIFICE AND CEREMONY
To please their gods, the Maya offered their own blood at special rites. Sometimes they also offered human lives. The Aztecs believed that their many gods needed human hearts to stay strong, and sacrificed thousands of people to them. Aztec and Mayan sacrifices were made before shrines on flat-topped pyramids, like that at Tikal in Guatemala (right). Mysterious picture writing has been found on some Mayan pyramids, and is now being translated.

INCA PYRAMID MOUNDS
The Incas ruled a vast area of South America in the fifteenth century AD. In the city of Cuzco in Peru they built a great temple called the Coricancha (right) to their sun-god, Inti. There they offered food and beer and sacrificed animals to their god.

THE MODERN MONUMENT
A pyramid made of glass (right) forms the new entrance to the Louvre Museum in Paris, France.

Did other peoples mummify their dead? Mummification is a very old practice in South America. Mummies of the Nazca people in Peru date from about 200 BC to AD 500. Human sacrifices were sometimes buried in the Andean mountains, where they were naturally preserved in the snow and ice.

REMEMBERING THE DEAD
Stone or ceramic funeral masks were used in the traditional funeral rites of several Native American peoples, in a way similar to that of the Egyptians.

NORTH AMERICA

Some Native North American peoples also built pyramids. The Mississippians built towns in AD 700-1500. The important buildings were set on great mounds of earth (above). Many peoples buried their dead in earth mounds with gifts and treasure.

A lasting impression

In modern times, many architects have used pyramid shapes and Egyptian decorations as part of their designs. In Las Vegas, USA, a huge casino based on the Great Pyramid has been built. It is the same size as Khufu's tomb, and is guarded by a giant Sphinx! Many decorations, such as those on the Empire State Building in New York or on these apartments in San Francisco, USA (below), are directly influenced by Egyptian pyramid paintings, while tiles and wallpaper often show decorative lotus or papyrus-leaf designs.

BIBLICAL BUILDINGS

The early peoples of Mesopotamia built mud-brick temples on platforms on the ruins of older temples. The platforms got taller over the years and became huge, stepped mounds similar to early pyramids.

We call them ziggurats. The great ziggurat Etemenanki was built by Nebuchadnezzar (604-561 BC) in Babylon, home of the famous Hanging Gardens. It might have inspired the story of the Tower of Babel (above).

The Lasting IMAGE

After Napoleon's expedition in 1798, a craze for ancient Egypt began. This happened again after the opening of the Suez Canal in 1869, and in 1922 with the discovery of the tomb of Tutankhamun. Each time, people collected Egyptian antiques and visited Egypt. Others bought Egyptian-style jewellery, furniture, buildings or ornaments (below). Egyptian images were used in all sorts of ways – even for things that had nothing to do with Egypt, like this make-up advertisement (right). Pyramid shapes and Egyptian decorations are still used in many products.

A LASTING FASHION
Middle Kingdom rulers also had pyramids, which were made of mud brick rather than stone. People realised that pyramids were easily robbed, so the New Kingdom rulers picked a remote valley – the Valley of the Kings – in which they cut rocky tombs. Pyramid power was not forgotten; the valley has a pyramid-shaped mountain towering above it. The workers who cut the rock built their own village at Deir-el-Medina. All their tombs had mini pyramids on top.

Is the Great Pyramid great? The sides are 229 m long, and the height just over 145 m. The base is so big that you could easily fit 8 football pitches on to it.

WHAT WERE THEY FOR?

A mosaic in St Mark's Cathedral, Italy, shows how people in the Middle Ages believed the pyramids to be ancient grain stores built by Joseph (of multi-coloured coat fame). They were shown with doors and windows, an idea found in several early books (see illustration at bottom of page, from 1694).

GRUESOME USES

In medieval Europe, many people believed that mummies had healing powers. They ground them into fine powder, which they mixed into medicines. The French King Francis I (below) swore by powdered mummy as a tonic! In the nineteenth century, mummy parts were used as ornaments, and mummy unwrappings were social events. Modern cryogenics allows people to be 'frozen' scientifically when they die, in the hope that they can be revived in the future.

Still more to discover?

Despite centuries of exploration and discovery, there are still a great number of mysteries to be solved. Many sites have yet to be excavated. For example, only recently the remains of Khufu's Valley Temple and an ancient bakery were unearthed, and in 1995 an amazing discovery was made in the Valley of the Kings – the rock-cut tombs of several sons of King Ramesses II. Every year, there are various new theories about how and why the pyramids were built. UPUAUT II has shown that there are still many undiscovered secrets. Will our ideas be proved right or wrong? Whatever happens, the mysteries of the pyramids will continue to intrigue people worldwide, for centuries to come.

TIME

c. 5000-3100 BC **Predynastic Period**
Upper & Lower Egypt formed

c. 3100-2686 BC **Archaic Period**
(Dynasties I-II)
Upper & Lower Egypt united

c. 2686-2150 BC **Old Kingdom**
(Dynasties III-VI)

c. 2686-2649 Zoser
c. 2680 Step Pyramid built
c. 2589-2566 Khufu
c. 2580 Great Pyramid built
c. 2666-2505 Khafre & Menkaure

c. 2150-2040 BC **First Intermediate Period**
(Dynasties VII-X)
Collapse of rule of the Kings

c. 2040-1640 BC **Middle Kingdom**
(Dynasties XI-XIII)
c. 2040 Egypt reunited

c. 1640-1552 BC **Second Intermediate Period (Dynasties XIV-XVII)**
Invasion by foreigners called Hyksos; they are later driven out

c. 1552-1085 BC **New Kingdom (Dynasties XVIII-XX)**
Kings buried in Valley of the Kings

c. 1085-664 BC **Third Intermediate
Period (Dynasties XXI-XXV)**

c. 664-332 BC **Late Period
(Dynasties XXVI-XXX)**
c. 525-404 & 341-332 Persians take Egypt

605-562 BC *City of Babylon rebuilt*

LINE

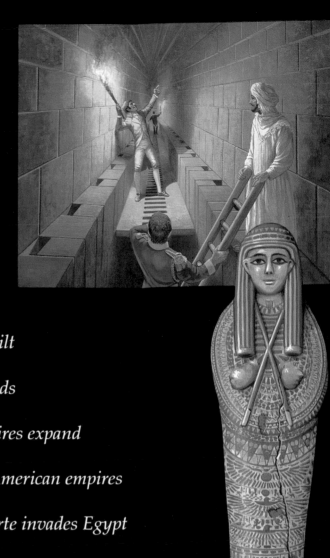

332 BC *Alexander the Great conquers Egypt*

323-30 BC *The Ptolemies rule Egypt*

30 BC *Egypt becomes part of Roman Empire*

AD **250-900** *Maya empire at its most powerful*

AD **639-642** *Arab forces invade and rule Egypt*

AD **700-1200** *North American mound cities built*

AD **950-1200** *Toltecs invade and rule Maya lands*

1400s *Aztec and Inca empires expand*

1500s *Spanish take S. American empires*

1798 *Napoleon Bonaparte invades Egypt*

1799 *Rosetta Stone discovered in N. Egypt*

1817 *Giovanni Caviglia opens Great Pyramid*

1822 *Hieroglyphs translated*

1850 *Auguste Mariette excavates Saqqara*

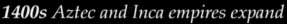

1880-81 *Petrie surveys all Giza pyramids*

1900-now *Excavations at Saqqara & Giza*

1922 *Tomb of Tutankhamun discovered*

1994 *UPUAUT II finds tiny door in Queen's chamber shaft of Great Pyramid at Giza*

1995 *Rock-cut tombs of several sons of Ramesses II discovered in Valley of the Kings*

INDEX

Picture credits (Abbreviations: t-top, m-middle, b-bottom, r-right, l-left): 4-5: Robert Harding Picture Library; 10t, 11t: Hulton Deutsch; 10b: Mary Evans Picture Library; 11b, 30b, 34: Frank Spooner Pictures; 12 both, 18, 22 both, 23, 25t: Courtesy of the Trustees of the British Museum, London; 25b, 35: Eye Ubiquitous; 30t: Courtesy of Rudolf Gantenbrink; 31, 39: Science Photo Library; 36: Roger Vlitos; 37: Hutchison Library.